Poems From A Prophetic Poet

Charles Haven Logan Sr.

WESTBOW
PRESS®
A DIVISION OF THOMAS NELSON
& ZONDERVAN

This book is a work of non-fiction. Unless otherwise noted, the author and the publisher make no explicit guarantees as to the accuracy of the information contained in this book and in some cases, names of people and places have been altered to protect their privacy.

WestBow Press books may be ordered through booksellers or by contacting:

WestBow Press
A Division of Thomas Nelson & Zondervan
1663 Liberty Drive
Bloomington, IN 47403
www.westbowpress.com
1 (866) 928-1240

Because of the dynamic nature of the Internet, any web addresses or links contained in this book may have changed since publication and may no longer be valid. The views expressed in this work are solely those of the author and do not necessarily reflect the views of the publisher, and the publisher hereby disclaims any responsibility for them.

Any people depicted in stock imagery provided by Getty Images are models, and such images are being used for illustrative purposes only. Certain stock imagery © Getty Images.

ISBN: 978-1-9736-7040-7 (sc)
ISBN: 978-1-9736-7041-4 (e)

Library of Congress Control Number: 2019910609

Print information available on the last page.

WestBow Press rev. date: 07/30/2019

A Friend

A friend is someone who is always there
To show you their love and care
A friend is someone in whom you can depend
Having a helping hand and warns you about sin
A friend corrects you when you are wrong
Through their love for God and loyalty helps keep you strong
A friend is someone who is always around
When the cares of this world knock you down
A friend will pick you up and dust you off and send you on your way
Stand in the gap on your behalf and will never cease to pray

A Day At Work

At work I begin to earnestly pray
That the Lord will guide and see me through today
I heard a voice from within me speak
Saying, I am strong, you are weak
So allow me to carry your load
So today's journey will not be a long weary road
I felt peace and joy arise from within
Knowing Jesus had purged me from my sin
My day turned out to blessed and easy
Because Jesus burden is light and always pleases

A Morning Prayer

I awaken each morning in prayer
Praying that God will always be there
Yes, praying that He will be here when I need Him most
Praying that He will always be close
If God moves, I feel that I will fall
But before we walked, we had to learn how to crawl
Yes, I am only a babe in Christ
But I constantly thank Him for giving me eternal life

A Trip to the Doctor

I went to the doctor for a back pain
I didn't realize it was so much to be gained
You see, God spoke clearly through this man
Doc told me exactly where he stands
He talked to me as a father talks to a son
He told me how my victory could be won
Doc told me what God loves and that is "TRUTH"
Now all I have to do is put it to good use

A True Friend

A true friend loves at all times and a brother is born for adversity
God puts friends together to show His love grace and mercy
A true friend recognizes that two are better than one
It's similar to our Heavenly Father and His only begotten Son
A true friend realizes that he cannot succeed alone
He needs true friends to build him up and make him strong
A true friend knows that he can find help in others
Recognizing true friends in Christ are
born again and sincere brothers
A true friend will always go the extra mile
They are pleasant and courageous and
distinguished by their godly smile

A True Shepherd

God has commissioned pastors to feed the flock
Jesus invested His life for productive stock
A true shepherd has the heart of God
He's diligent which guarantees the very best rewards
A shepherd takes heed to know what state the flock is in
Teaching them to always seek God and warn them about sin
A true shepherd loves to teach
Counsel and minister to the sheep
Believing God for uncommon perfection and the souls
He will always keep
A true shepherd can be summed up in a few words
He loves sheep, is a good example and is always
A blessing to be heard

An Unseen Force From Within

In the fear of the Lord is strong confidence
God moves through an unseen force from within
Producing great evidence
It's God who works in us to do of His will and good pleasure
It is deep and worth more than any found treasure
Our lives are in God's hands as shapeable clay
He breaks, molds and shapes us along life's way
It's an awesome thing to see God's handiwork
It's amazing how He can take us and make us from dirt
I am blessed to be on the Master's potter's wheel
Learning when to move and when to stand still

Applying God's Word

There is a way that seems right unto a man
However, the end thereof is the way of death
Thank God for His promise of prosperity in my soul
And His divine health
God has the answer for everything the devil tries to do
It's just a matter of whose eyes we choose to look through
As we look to God for everything we need
We'll begin to understand His plan for us to succeed
It takes time to build on the things of God
That's why His word is quick and powerful
And sharper than any two-edged sword
So let's begin to apply the word of God
To our days and in our lives
As He cleanses our hearts delivering us from every wicked device

Being Attentive to God's Word

We must not only be hearers, but doers of God's word
Speaking with authority and being bold with being heard
God wants us to be fruitful and multiply
While He gets our new homes ready, beyond the sky
God wants us to capture His thoughts and obey
This will help keep a lot of stumbling blocks out of our way
The main thing we must do
Be attentive to God's word our whole life through

Blessings From Above

I will always give God all the praise
Because He has really changed my ways
We should continuously praise our Father's name
Because in our lives, He's made a miraculous change
God wants us to walk in perfect love
That's why He sends His blessings from above
So let's try with all our might
To keep God pleased and do what's right

Casting All My Care

In this world of trials and temptations
The Lord is always there to give us great expectations
The more I go through the closer I get
To those divine blessings that I can't regret
The Lord uses tests to bring us up in Him
It's like a basketball player who loves the gym
As I go through afflictions, toils and snares
I've learn to cast all my cares upon Him
For only He can bear

Count Time in the Penitentiary

When it is count time in the penitentiary
God knows this is essential
Everyone must definitely be accounted for
That's why the officers go from door to door
I hope and pray that no one tries to escape
Because we shouldn't be like Jonah, making God wait
We can run but cannot hide from God
Because He knew our intentions from the start

Fellowship

I thank God for my fellow Christians
Not only do they talk about God, they also listen
God wants us to fellowship with each other
Because in Christ, we are all brothers
I enjoy seeing that glow in their faces
Even though most of us are from different places
I look forward to being home in Glory divine
With all Christian brothers and God on our minds

From Glory To Glory

We must be doers of the word and not hearers only
This will stop us from being hypocrites and phonies
In life we must make vital decisions and choices
Through God's guidance we'll make the right ones knowing His voice
As we meditate on God's word day and night
Our lives will be joyful and full of spiritual delights
The word of God is a lamp unto our feet
And always lights our paths
Giving us much needed strength
As God stands on our behalf
As we continue to build on God's word of truth
We'll be witnesses of putting His word to proper use
God's word should be reflected on our faces
As He takes us from glory to glory by His amazing grace

God Flows In Us

We're commanded to be wise as serpents, harmless as doves
As God's spirit flows through us from up above
God is high and yet has respect unto the lowly
It's just a matter of trusting Him as All-knowing
We can't see God, however, He's everywhere
He knows our every thought and truly cares
God wants us to be willing to trust His word
Knowing he speaks to us from within silently
And is strongly heard

God Is In Charge

The Lord is our spiritual leader and King
Not just in heaven but over everything
The Lord made the oceans and the seas
That's why we should learn to walk on our knees
The Lord made the laws upon the land
God has everything in the palm of His hands
So we should accept Jesus before it's too late
If we have plans of walking through those pearly gates

God Restores Our Souls

I often sit here in my cell
Constantly thanking for saving me from hell
I'm overjoyed with God restoring my soul
And filling me with self-control
I know that God wants me to continuously maintain
For me to live is Christ and to die is gain
That's why I confess my sins because He is faithful and just
That's why serving God to me, is a must

God Takes Care of His Children

God allows us to go to prison for a reason
God has shown me this is only for a season
Because He wants us to put Him first
Through our faithfulness, honesty and prayers
He quenches our thirst
God doesn't want any of His children in jail
That's why He holds the keys to the locks
At any time, He can go our bail
This is God's way of strengthening His own
While He watches with patience from His mighty throne

God's Always Near

Jesus paved the way for you and me
All we need is faith, trust and belief
God put us under His angels
If we live right, we'll be free from danger
We have Satan's angels on our left shoulders
A God's angels on our right
That's why Jesus is here for our fight
There're always two voices we hear
One far away and one near
It's up to us to make the right choice
And always acknowledge our Fathers voice

God's Best

God allows us to be tried in the spiritual fire
The carnal side of us must die
The trying of our faith is more precious than gold
God wants us purified deep down in our souls
The key to us surviving each and every test
It's based upon our willingness to have God's best
It takes time, patience and world overcoming faith
God is building us into spiritual sprinters in His race
So relax and enjoy the ride
God is developing everything we need on the inside

God's Blessing

God has anointed me to write poems
Something that I really enjoy doing
God blesses all of us differently
All we need is awareness to see
God has special blessings for us all
If we would soften our hearts and answer His call
God wants all of us to receive our blessings
However, unfortunately
It's usually after we've learned an expensive lesson

God's Grace

God's grace is always sufficient for me
Through times of severe trials, tests and misery
God's presence is where we experience fullness of joy
It's similar to a child on Christmas day with a brand new toy
This is all a part of something we can learn
It's just a matter of growing spiritually so we can clearly discern
God's grace is always within our reach
That's why in the spirit we never need a breach
God's grace helps us to keep a constant pace
As we enjoy our heaven bound race

God's Insight

Believing what God said is accepting
And trusting Him is depending
Our God so awesome
Declaring the ending from the beginning
The word of God is true and every man should try it
As the Holy Spirit keep that holy fire lit
God never intended for us to be alone
His word is our comfort, strength and keeps us strong
Let's renew our minds to God's word of truth
Striving for perfection and putting it to its proper use
The entrance of God's word gives light
Causing us to have His vision and Godly sight

God's Never Too Busy

We can always call God and have a serious talk
He will never say "It's your fault"
God looks forward to hearing our humble cry
While here on earth, until the day we day
He is a very jealous God
That's why He wants us to stay on one accord
God wants us to have peace, joy, happiness and love
While He guides us down below
From heaven above

God's Way of Living

I was once filled with anger and sadness
But God has taken away that madness
God is showing me all about His way of living
You see, God is all about spiritual giving
He's shown me through prayer how to seek His help
This way, close to His heart, He must always be kept
The Lord wants us to put everything in His hands
So on solid ground we will always be able to stand

Godly Connections

It's very important that we connect with those of God
Knowing that two are better than one
And they receive a great reward
We sharpen each other as iron sharpens iron
Striving together for perfection through renewed minds
Our past begins to vanish and our future looks bright
For we know God's our bright and morning star
And our shining light
The right timing and connections always lead to success
For by God's grace we are delivered from this worldliness
We come together in the spirit as one
Reflecting God's image from His only begotten Son
So let's stay connected in spirit and in truth
Things that don't apply let them fly
Those that do put them to good use

Godly Relationships

God wants us to be in the right relationships
Knowing that prosperous lives are developed
Through godly friendships
We must desire to grow together as one
As our heavenly Father is with His Son
A relationship that's based on thought instead of chance
This will build godly character and help us advance
Life is what you make it and who you chose to assist
Knowing God's anointing makes us tight
As cement inside of bricks
Be sure to connect with those who build you
Causing us in life, to be honest, have integrity and operate in truth
Godly relationships take time to establish, develop and grow
That's why we must humble ourselves, bind together
And move with a godly flow

God's Divine Grace

The name of the Lord is a strong tower
The righteous runs into Him and are safe
This is all a part of God's divine grace
God is always available and never puts us on hold
For Jesus is the Author and finisher of our faith
He's the Bishop and Shepherd of our soul
God is always near, even the confession of our mouth
Faith in God rids us of all anxiety, fears and doubts
Let's begin to call on the Lord in sincerity at all times
Knowing that He desires us to be prosperous
Because we're always on His mind
God knows what we need before we ask
It's just our willingness to invite His influence
Allowing Him to handle every task

He'll Always Come Through

I'm very encouraged as I wait on the Lord
Knowing that His gifts are perfect and come from the heart
Our God knows what we need before we cry out
It's our faith that pleases Him and destroys all doubts
As I wait on the Lord, I began to see Him for who He is
It's only because of His only begotten Son, that I live
There are always great rewards for waiting patiently
As the awesome anointing of God opens our eyes to see
Then just as He promised, He'll always come through
He's not a man that He should lie and He is always true

He's Always On Time

God is never late, He's always on time
This is why we must think like He does, possessing Jesus' mind
I marvel at God's season, timing and purpose
Knowing that He is our guide and deliverer and is there for us
God hears our prayers when we take time to call on Him
He has already declared the ending from the beginning
Our faith pleases God and causes Him to always respond
Isn't it awesome how our victory has already been won

He's Always There

The supernatural joy of the Lord is our strength
Keeping us strong within is God's intent
We must appreciate and value His presence
Knowing that in His face it's always pleasant
God enjoys us coming to spend quality time
This helps us stay focused and keep spiritual minds
It's a blessing to go to God in prayer
He's our Heavenly Father, Jehovah Shammah
And He's always there

Higher Ground

God gives us two ears and one mouth
So we can think about the things we say
Having others to realize
That life is not just a game we play
Our focus should be on what God wants us to do
And to Him we should always be true
God's plan for our lives always produces eternal things
If only to His words, we would always cling
God has what we need and it's easy to be found
It's just a matter of wanting it and seeking higher ground

I'm Blessed

The Lord keeps on blessing me
Which helps carry me through life's miseries
I am blessed in so many ways
That's why I give God all the praise
He blesses me going out and coming in
Most importantly, He died for my sins
I am blessed night and day
As the Lord continues to keep me from going astray

I'm Yours Lord

I'm yours Lord, willing to obey
As I attentively hear what you say
It's my faith that pleases you
As you show me what to do
I pursue and attain precious gifts
That always encourages and my spirit they lift
I'm yours Lord to use as please
Knowing the spiritual key is found
From strength on my knees

In His Presence

God will show us the path of life
For all the wrong, He'll make it right
We may feel hopeless and in despair
I may seems as if no one even cares
All alone and not knowing what to do
In fear and doubt and so confused
We may be weak, yet God will make us strong
He gives us the strength to keep going on
We can trust Him with all our soul
We must let Him have complete control
We can call on Him while He is near
Because in Him there is no fear
In His presence there is fullness of joy
At His right hand there are pleasures forevermore

It's All Worth It

My experience on the road to Damascus
Would now be considered a modern day classic
I was blessed to hear the voice I'd long to hear
Only by grace which has now brought Godly fear
God watched over and protected me
Even when I was spiritually blind and could not see
My ears are now open and receptive to what I hear
Knowing that God is Jehovah Shammah and is always near
God is a God of His season, time and purpose
For it is God that worketh in and through us
Which makes it all worth it

Let Us Love One Another
with God's Love

Let us love one another, for love is of God
Not with our mouth and lips but from the depths of our hearts
Man looks outwardly but God ponders the heart
That's why through faith working by love
We receive our ultimate reward
Love is an action that causes us to reach, touch and hold
To our confession of faith
Which will always help us to overcome envy, strife and hate
My prayer is that all God's true children
Knows Him for who He is
Living a life of love, peace and joy, demonstrating what God gives
The righteousness of God is revealed from faith to faith
Humbling ourselves praying constantly as we seek His face
Trusting our omnipotent all powerful God
For using us for His glory and allowing us to be a part

My Blessed Trip To Jail

It was a blessed trip to jail on May 27, 1991
Not realizing at the time, I was going to meet God's only Son
I began to call my family and friends about my release
Not knowing, it was God's time to give the spiritual increase
I began to learn and meditate on the things of God
As He transformed my life, setting me up for many rewards
I stood before the judge in August of this year
Filled with many anxieties, worries and fears
He gave me fifteen years, however, I knew I wasn't alone
For I had decided to allow Jesus to be on the throne
I was sent to Perry Correctional Institution to R & E
Where I began to learn the power in my knees
I went to no less than eight institutions
Being used of God to impart, strengthen and build godly constitutions
I missed parole twice, which I didn't understand
I felt much better when I put everything in God's hand
I was released on parole in December 1996
Allowing God to shape, mold, prepare and
put me back into societies mix
I stand strong today by the grace of God
My life is complete, free from every void

My Purpose

My purpose is to win souls for the Lord
Reaching out for Jesus with a two-edged sword
The Lord has given me an evangelistic anointing
Winning souls for Christ is never disappointing
I may water, someone else may plant
It's God who gives the increase, you can count on it
It's very important we know what God has chosen us to do
This is all a part of our minds being renewed
As we seek God's face and not His hand
He will begin to show us His holy divine plan

Our Place In The Kingdom

God's word commands us to be fruitful and multiply
This gives us that heavenly connection beyond the sky
God wants us to learn how to spiritually sow
Into the lives of others for their spiritual growth
As we draw nigh to God, He draws nigh to us
We begin to see how He longs to give us His anointed touch
Our life is hidden in God in Christ who is our life
Thank God for blessing us to be a part of Jesus' sacrifice
Our place in the kingdom of God is not to be taken lightly
For the Holy Spirit will teach us how to divide the word rightly
I'm blessed to be at the place in my Christian journey
Soaking up and applying God's word of truth to my life
Not just forever learning

Our Shepherd

The Lord is our shepherd
In Him we have everything we need
God's teachers taught us how to pray and read
We must trust God for our protection
For He is our true heaven connection
We should praise God because He does what's right
He takes care of us morning, noon and every night

Our Spiritual Fight

I choose to stay on the spiritual battlefield for my Almighty God
Fighting spiritual wickedness in the heavenlies
With a two-edged sword
My battle is not based on what I see
It's based on casting down every imagination that exalts itself
Against God's divine knowledge in me
In our fight for God what we say determines what God does
That why we call the things that be not as if it was
The battleground starts in the mind
God always move in His own time
Let's stay focus and endure to the end
As we use God's word in the battles, we always win

Our Supplier

The promises of God are yea and amen
To the glory of the Father by us
God looks for faith on the earth
Which always developes trust
We are commanded to trust God
And not lean to our own understanding
For God is someone who can be trusted
And is never too demanding
It brings joy to God's heart to see us succeed
Knowing that He is El Shaddai
And supplies all our needs

Our True and Just God

Our heavenly Father is always true and just
Through Jesus' blood and the word builds trust
God is a strong tower and we have a resting place
Which is very much needed in our heaven bound race
We must learn to depend on the wisdom of God
As we seek Jesus and press for His high mark
It is to our advantage to be willing and obey
As we humble ourselves, seeking His face night and day
As we grow in grace and knowledge of our Lord Jesus Christ
We learn by waiting, being alert and accepting His advice
Our hearts are fixed and our minds are changed
As we recognize it is God's will for us to be strange
Knowing that too often we look at what we see
That's why we must be students of God's word
Which constantly builds our faith, trust and belief

Praising God Daily

I pray to Almighty God when I wake up each morning
Praising God is part of my spiritual growing
I pray to God on my way to work each day
Praying that with Him I will always stay
I come to my room at lunch and fall on my knees
I feel that doing this will keep God pleased
I try to keep God close to me everywhere I go
While He watches from above down here below

Preparation Time

When the enemy comes in like a flood
God's anointing within us always lifts us from above
God declares the ending from the beginning
There's always preparation time before our sending
We are to be strong in the Lord and in the power of His might
Loving Jesus as He blots all our sins out of sight
We are not to be ignorant of Satan's devices
It's just a matter of wisdom by walking God's light
Our tests and trials come to make us strong
Knowing that we are of God and are
Being prepared for our heavenly home
We that are strong are commanded to
Bear the infirmities of the weak
This process starts with humility, patience
And the willingness to our God to make us whole and complete

PRICELESS

I thought about You as I walked today
Knowing You are there and guiding my way
You give me strength to carry on
Knowing it's Your love for me that keeps me strong
I've learned to recognize who You are
No matter where I am, You are never afar
I long to see You face to face
To thank You for your saving grace
However, while I'm here on this earth
I'll always value and appreciate Your priceless worth

Quieting the Storm

It hurts my heart so dearly
When some of the saints refuse to see so clearly
The power of God to save, heal and deliver today
If we humble ourselves, seek His face and pray
God has all power to quiet every storm
Keeping His own from life's troubles and harm
It's in His presence we find fullness of joy
It's similar to a child on Christmas Day with a desired toy
I find my faith in God increasing more
For it's in the trials and toils of life
When our character is developed and we grow

Serving God for Who He Is

What we ask God for is not our God but Jesus is
It's just a matter of us keeping it real
God always hears His children's request
He will always give us the very best
Let's not forget what He's already done
Giving us victorious lives through His only Son
Let's stay focus on the things above
So we will always cherish and appreciate God's agape love
Material things will always come and go
It's that inward connection with God
That builds character and causes spiritual growth
So let's always serve God for the right reasons
Knowing He's the same no matter what the season

Stay In Faith

I must always stay in faith
As I continue to run this heaven bound race
Faith is the key that unlocks heaven's door
As the Lord moves by His spirit and lets us know
Faith is what it takes to move God
As He hears our prayers and they touch His heart
As our faith grows from day to day
Lets walk in love and always obey

Students of the Word

Ignorance is as contagious as knowledge
That's why we must be students of the word in spiritual college
As we get off the milk of God's word and on to the meat
We realize God's desire is to fill, heal and make us complete
As we grow in God and the spiritual things
We'll have an appetite for God's word
To do it and we will cling
We'll begin to hunger and thirst for righteousness
Through meditation and study of the word
We will experience great success
Promotion doesn't come from the east, west, north or south
It comes from the words flowing from God's mouth

Thank You Father

Thank you Heavenly Father for your word is true
Thank you for loving me my whole life through
Thank you for sacrificing your only begotten Son
Thank you for the victory has been won
Thank you Father for in truth I now stand
Thank you for always extending your loving hands
As I now close on paper but never in worship and praise
Take my heart, mind, spirit and soul
And fill them with your godly ways

The Flesh Is A Mess

It is dangerous to walk in the flesh
Lord knows it only leads to a mess
That way that seems right leads to destruction
That's why it's important to follow God's instructions
Always wear the whole armor of God
As you press toward the most ultimate reward
The flesh only deals with our emotions
That's why it's very, very important
To have a personal devotion
In ending, it's important that I say
Keep the flesh under and do things Godly way

The Full Armor of God

If we let God work His will in our lives
We will have what it takes to survive
That's why we should wear the
Full armor of God wherever we go
So He will fill us with the Holy Spirit and we will grow
It's not what goes into the body but what comes out
God wants us to be filled with confidence and have no doubts
In essence, I think what God really wants to say
Is that we should serve Him constantly and always obey

There is No Other

God is our refuge and strength a very present help in trouble
To know Him, we can depend, for there is no other
I believe God anticipates our need for help
That's why the word of God is precious
And in our hearts it must be kept
Our God is high, yet has respect upon the lowly
He takes our lives and builds great character
From our life's story
It's awesome to have a God who knows
The ending from the beginning
If we would realize the power we have in our knees
While we are bending

True Confession from the Heart

Repentance is the golden hinge that opens
The door to the next seasons of blessings in your life
God knows when we're wrong
And He knows when we're right
God longs to hear us when we confess our wrong to Him
It's very similar to a dusty gem
Sometimes sin comes slow, however, sure
It's up to us to agree we've sinned and desire to be pure
We are to blossom into awesome saints of God
This process begins with true confessions from the heart

Walking With God
Around the Track

I enjoy walking around the penitentiary track
Praying constantly that God takes me around and back
As I walk, I am blessed to be able to witness to others
Because God's word says if we are born again
We are all brothers
God lets the sun shine bright sometimes
This puts God only on our mind
You see, God wants us to appreciate His works
While He strengthens us and keeps us alert

We Need God's Help

I go to church as much as I can
I want God to know where I stand
I'm trying to let God know I appreciate what He's done
By accepting me as a long lost son
It took 34 years for me to make the right step
Now I thank God for His help
I don't know what God is changing me to be
But I'm learning to be patient, to wait and see

When God Speaks

It's important when God speaks
For us to practice the very things we teach
We should wait on God to confirm
What we must do on His terms
It's so easy we often find ways to make it hard
It's not a matter whether we're dumb or smart
It's a matter of knowing God's voice
Which should always cause us to make the right choice
So let's begin to focus on the things God says
So He can lead, guide and teach us His godly ways

Who Is a True Father

A Our Heavenly Father is always true
He always inspires us for His good use
A father should always be head of the household
He should share in the responsibility for our souls
A true father has compassion and love
He is caring and instills precious qualities from above
He understands the position he's in
Being a good example and warning us about sin
Who is a true father
One that's born of the spirit and the water

Who's Building It?

Except the Lord build the house
They labor in vain that built it
God wants to build us
Through the power of the Holy Spirit
God builds us so that others will know
The only way they got here, is through spiritual growth
God's plan is out of this world
As we reach higher in the spirit and deeper in His word
It's a blessing to watch God take what we have
And transform it into life
Freeing us from toils, snares, envy and strife
Let's use what we have for God's glory
So once we're in heaven
We'll have a legacy from our life's story

Witnessing

I love to witness for the Lord
This is a gift that originates from the heart
There are two kinds of witnesses God uses for His glory
The most powerful one is hidden in your life's story
What we do always speaks louder than what we say
Your life coupled with godly fear causes you to be willing to obey
When people see your light shining
They often want to hear who you know
This comes from practicing the word of God
As He causes us to grow
As I witness to others I often think about where
God has brought me from
Having been a wretched man, lost and undone
Witnessing is something I look forward to do
As the master Potter puts my life together making me brand new